MAPPING EARTHFORMS

Coasts

Melanie Waldron

Heinemann Library
Chicago, Illinois

© 2008 Heinemann Library
a division of Reed Elsevier Inc.
Chicago, Illinois

Customer Service 888-454-2279
Visit our Web site at www.heinemannraintree.com

Designed by Richard Parker and Q2A solutions
Illustrations: Jeff Edwards
Picture Research: Hannah Taylor
Production: Duncan Gilbert

Originated by Chroma Graphics (Overseas) Pte. Ltd
Printed and Bound in China by Leo Paper Group

11 10 09 08 07
10 9 8 7 6 5 4 3 2 1

ISBNs: 978-1-4034-9605-8 (hardcover)
        978-1-4034-9615-7 (paperback)

Library of Congress Cataloging-in-Publication Data

Waldron, Melanie.
  Coasts / Melanie Waldron.
      p. cm. -- (Mapping earthforms)
  Includes bibliographical references and index.
  ISBN 978-1-4034-9605-8 (library binding - hardback) -- ISBN
978-1-4034-9615-7 (library binding - pbk.) 1. Coasts--Juvenile literature.
I. Title.
  GB453.W35 2007
  508.314'6--dc22

                            2007003573

Acknowledgments
The publishers would like to thank the following for permission to reproduce photographs: Alamy Images/David Wall p. 11; Corbis pp. 15 (Bill Ross), 10 (Steve Terrill), 5 (Torleif Svensson), 23 (Yann Arthus-Bertrand), 7 (zefa/Theo Allofs); FLPA/D P Wilson p. 8; Getty Images/Stone p. 27; naturepl.com pp. 19 (Ben Osborne), 18 (Christophe Courteau); NHPA pp. 16 (Alberto Nardi), 17 (Jim Bain); Photolibrary pp. 4 (Pacific Stock), 26 (Photononstop); Science Photo Library pp. 20 (Peter Bowater), 9 (William Ervin); Skyscan/ J Farmarp p. 13; Still Pictures pp. 12 (Jeff Greenburg), 24 (Pierre Zeni).

Cover photograph reproduced with permission of Lonely Planet/Richard I'Anson

Disclaimer
All the Internet addresses (URLs) given in this book were valid at the time of going to press. However, due to the dynamic nature of the Internet, some addresses may have changed, or sites may have changed or ceased to exist since publication. While the author and publishers regret any inconvenience this may cause readers, no responsibility for any such changes can be accepted by either the author or publishers.

Contents

Any words appearing in the text in bold, **like this**, are explained in the Glossary. You can find the answers to Map Active questions on page 29.

What Is a Coast?

Think of a place where the land meets the sea. You might think of a sunny, sandy beach where the waves gently wash onto the shore. You might think of a steep, rocky cliff with huge, white waves crashing against black rocks. Both of these places are coasts. Coasts are everywhere that the land and sea meet.

There are many different types of coasts all over the world. But they all have one thing in common—the sea. All coasts are affected by waves and **tides**, and all coasts change because of the sea. They might change every day, as the tides come in or go out. Or the change could take hundreds of years, as the sea **erodes** the land. The powerful action of the sea means that coasts are the world's most rapidly changing landforms.

▼ The sea can be very powerful and can attack the coastline. Hard rock can resist this attack, but softer rock will soon give way.

▲ Coasts can be very busy places! Most people love to spend time by the sea. However, this means that coasts can sometimes be badly affected by human activity.

How have coasts formed?

For the last 6,000 years, sea levels around the world have been stable. Coastlines have been developing and changing along the edges of all the **continents** of the world. The coastlines you see today have formed during this time. They are a result of the **interaction** between the land and the sea. In some places the sea washes away the land, and in others it builds up the land.

Life at the coast

There are many different types of plants and animals living at the coast. Many of these have **adapted** to living in the narrow strip where the land meets the sea. Plants and animals have done this in order to survive in this changing environment. Humans also live and work at the coast, and we are affecting coastlines all around the world.

Coasts of the World

Coasts are found all over the world, wherever a land mass meets the sea. Most countries in the world have some coastline, but some do not. There are 43 countries that are **landlocked**. This means that they do not have any land that borders the sea. Paraguay in South America, for example, is landlocked. All other countries have at least part of their border meeting the sea. Some countries, such as Iceland, are completely surrounded by the sea. The whole border is made up of coastline.

In some countries, the coastline can change quickly over a short distance. In the United Kingdom, for example, some parts of the south coast change from rocky cliffs to flat bays, concrete sea defenses, and shingle beaches in less than 31 miles (50 kilometers). In other parts of the world, however, the same type of coast can stretch for long distances. The Skeleton Coast in Namibia, for example, is a huge area of sand and sea that stretches for more than 310 miles (500 kilometers) up the West African coast.

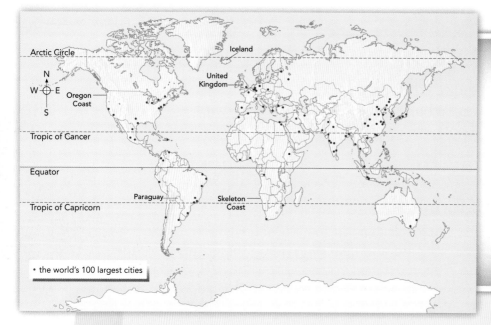

• the world's 100 largest cities

◀ Most of the world's largest cities are found very close to the coast. One reason is that access to the sea makes it easy for trade in that area.

MAP ACTIVE

Can you identify any areas in the world where there are no large cities near the coast? Think of some possible reasons for this.

The most important factors that shape the coastline are the rock that the land is made of and the direction and power of the waves. Very hard rocks, such as granite, are able to resist attack from powerful waves, although over time they eventually **erode**. When hard rocks erode, they can leave behind some amazing landforms. Waves can easily erode soft rock, such as clay. As the land erodes, the coastline can quickly move inward. The material that has been eroded may move along the coast and change the coastline there.

In very cold areas of the world, such as northern Russia, where the land and sea are covered with ice, it is quite difficult to tell where the coastline is. The coastline is visible only in summer, when some of the ice has melted.

▲ The Skeleton Coast in Namibia was named for the dangerous rocks and powerful waves that lie off the shore. Many ships have been wrecked along this coast.

Tides and Waves

Tides

Every coastline around the world is affected by the changing **tide**. The tide is the rise and fall in the surface of the sea. Twice every day the sea level is high, and the sea washes higher up on the land. This is called **high tide**. As soon as it reaches high tide, the sea starts to drop down again until it reaches its lowest level. This is called **low tide**. At low tide, the sea does not wash as high on the land. Low tides also occur twice every day.

high tide

low tide

▲ Plants and animals living in the area between high tide and low tide are specially **adapted**. They are able to cope with being under the sea for half their lives.

The tides are created by the pull of the Moon's **gravity** on the sea. As the Moon orbits Earth, it pulls a bulge of water with it. This action creates the tides. The difference in height between high tide and low tide can be large, depending on the position of the Moon and the shape of the coastline. In some places the difference can be more than 33 feet (10 meters).

▲ As waves head toward the coast, the bottom of the wave begins to drag on the ground below the sea. This makes the top of the wave break, or topple over.

Waves

The surface of the sea is rarely smooth and still. This is because of waves. Waves are created by winds blowing over the sea's surface. Stronger winds create higher, more powerful waves with lots of energy. The waves can build up in height and energy if the wind blows in the same direction over a large distance. We call this distance the **fetch**. The longer the fetch is, the larger the wave.

Waves can have a huge effect on the coast. Small waves with little energy wash gently onto the land. These waves do not create much **erosion**. However, large waves with lots of energy can crash onto the land, breaking up bits of rock and moving them around. The wind and the size and power of the waves can change a coast from a calm and peaceful place to a wild and dangerous one.

Erosion at the Coast

Waves and erosion

Wherever waves break on the coast, they can cause **erosion** of rock. The amount of erosion depends on the height and strength of the waves, and also on the type of rock.

There are different types of erosion:
- **Abrasion** — Waves can contain particles of sand and **shingle**. When the waves hit the rock, the particles wear the rock away.
- **Wave pounding** — When strong, high waves slam against the rock, the energy of the wave produces a shock wave through the rock. This can cause it to weaken and eventually break up.
- **Hydraulic pressure** — Little holes and cracks on the surface of rocks have air inside them. This air can become **compressed** when the waves hit the rocks. The trapped air can cause the cracks to get bigger. This action breaks up the rock.
- **Corrosion** — Some types of rock, such as limestone, dissolve in salty seawater. Over time the rock gets worn farther and farther back.

Landforms of erosion

Erosion at the coast can create some amazing landforms. **Headlands** and **bays** form when the rock type changes from hard to soft along the coast. Headlands are sections of hard rock, such as granite, that stick out into the sea. Bays in between the headlands are areas of soft rock, such as clay, that have been more easily **eroded**.

▶ The sea has eroded the rock near Crook Point in Oregon to leave behind these amazing formations.

▲ At Noosa Head in Queensland, Australia, the sea has eroded the soft rock to form bays. The harder rock has resisted erosion to form headlands. This shows that the rock type has a great effect on the shape of the coast.

Wave-cut platforms are found at the bottom of coastal cliffs. They form when the waves erode the bottom of the cliff, and the cliff above collapses. Over time the cliff is pushed farther and farther back, leaving a flat platform of rock that is exposed at low tide.

The most amazing coastal landforms include caves, **arches**, and **stacks**. All of these are created over long periods of time as waves gradually erode more and more material. Caves can be worn through to the other side, leaving an archway. If the rock at the top of the archway collapses, this leaves a stack standing on its own in the sea.

11

Deposition at the Coast

Longshore drift

When rocks are **eroded**, the small particles that break off can be carried in the waves. Over time, these particles get worn and rounded to form sand or **shingle**. Waves can pick up this sand or shingle and move it along the coast.

Longshore drift occurs when waves hit the coast at an angle, instead of straight up and down. These waves pick up material and move it up the beach. Then, when the waves wash back down the beach, they move in a straight line rather than at an angle. This means that the material does not move back to its original position. Over time this causes lots of material to move to a new position along the beach.

▼ Longshore drift can build up material in some places, but in other places material is constantly being removed. On some beaches, **beach replenishment** can help reduce the effects of longshore drift.

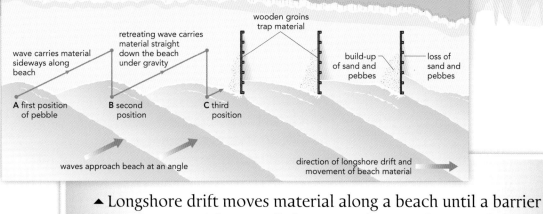

- **A** first position of pebble

wave carries material sideways along beach

retreating wave carries material straight down the beach under gravity

- **B** second position

wooden groins trap material

- **C** third position

build-up of sand and pebbes

loss of sand and pebbes

waves approach beach at an angle

direction of longshore drift and movement of beach material

▲ Longshore drift moves material along a beach until a barrier stops the material, or until the coast changes shape and the waves no longer approach at an angle.

Landforms of deposition

Waves drop particles of sand and shingle in a process called **deposition**. Deposition takes place when waves reach more sheltered areas of coast, where they lose their energy and can no longer carry the material. Deposition can create some beautiful landforms.

Spits are long, narrow stretches of sand and shingle. They are joined to the coastal land at one end. Spits form when beach material is moved along the coast until it reaches areas where the coast changes shape and the wave energy drops. A spit that reaches another section of coastal land is called a **bar**.

A **tombolo** is a stretch of sand and shingle that joins an offshore island to the mainland. It is created when the waves break against the sea side of the island, then curve around the island. As the waves curve around, they lose their energy. The material is dropped where the waves have the lowest energy.

Barrier islands are made of deposited sand and shingle. They form long stretches of islands running alongside the coastline. Often **salt marshes** build up behind these islands. Salt marshes are areas of deposited mud, **silt**, and sand that have been built up high enough to allow specially **adapted** plants to grow.

▶ Dawlish Warren in Devon, England, is a spit that has built up over hundreds of years. The sea is constantly moving material along the coast.

The Oregon Coast

The state of Oregon lies on the western side of the United States. The coastline of Oregon stretches for 296 miles (476 kilometers) along the Pacific Ocean. There are some sandy beaches along the coast, but it is most famous for its rocky cliffs and shores. Lighthouses all along the coast warn ships about these rocks.

Erosion has played a large part in shaping the Oregon coast. There are rocky **headlands**, sea **stacks**, **arches**, and caves. In the central part there are large **sand dunes**, formed by the wind blowing sand into huge mounds.

Coastal wildlife

There are many different **species** of plants and animals living along the Oregon coast. Sea lions, seals, whales, and porpoises make their homes in the coastal waters. Seabirds such as the tufted puffin and the western gull feed on the rich variety of small sea life. The **tide pools** contain a whole range of animals from sea urchins to crabs. Plant life includes the coastal strawberry (a type of rose) and the beach daisy.

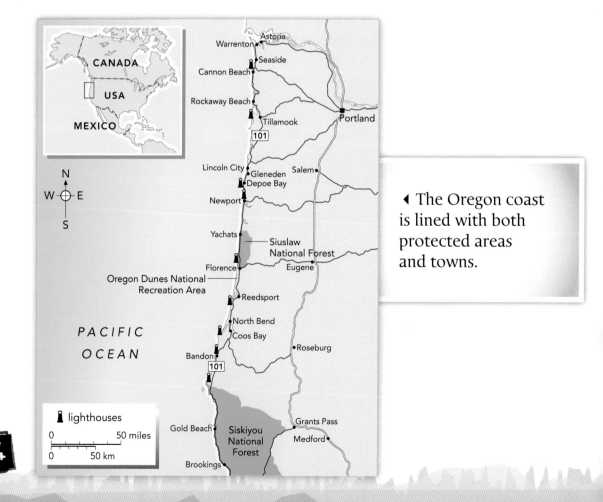

◄ The Oregon coast is lined with both protected areas and towns.

▲ Cannon Beach on the Oregon coast is a good example of the rocky natural beauty of the area.

People of the Oregon coast

More than 10,000 years ago, Native Americans settled along the coast. They fished the seas using wooden canoes and hunted the land nearby. After Europeans began visiting and trading in the 1700s, the first permanent town, Astoria, was built in the early 1800s. Soon settlements were being built all along the coast, as people took advantage of the good farming land, the rich timber forests, and the growing salmon-fishing industry.

Today tourism is a very important industry on the Oregon coast. Tourists come to see the spectacular natural rock formations along the coast, to relax on sandy beaches, and to visit old fishing villages and bigger resorts. More energetic activities are also offered—including surfing, boating, scuba-diving, fishing, cycling, and hiking. However, there is a downside to the popularity of the area. There is only one major road, Highway 101, that runs the length of the coastline, and traffic jams are very common. In fact, the area has been named as having the worst tourist traffic in the United States.

Coastal Plants

All plants growing at the coast have to cope with some fairly harsh conditions. Plants that grow where seawater sometimes covers the land must be able to grow in salty water. On many coasts there are strong winds, and these winds can pick up salty spray from the sea that then blows onto plant leaves. Plants have **adapted** to living and growing in these environments.

▲ Coastal vegetation has adapted to deal with changing tides, salty air and water, and strong winds.

Halophytes

In coastal areas where **silt** is deposited—for example, where a river meets the sea—plants can grow on the **mudflats** that form. These areas of mud are located in what is known as the **intertidal zone** (the land that is exposed at **low tide** but covered by the sea at **high tide**). Plants that grow here are called **halophytes**. Halophytes can survive in salty conditions that would kill other plants. Halophytes include saltbush and cordgrass.

▲ Halophytes such as this marsh samphire have adapted to living in very salty conditions. Marsh samphire can be eaten. It must be washed carefully and then boiled in water for around ten minutes.

Halophytes can control the balance of salt in their tissues in two main ways. Some plants are called excluders. They have special **cells** inside them that can collect the salt and pull it out through the plant's leaves. Other plants are called includers. These plants store large quantities of water inside their cells so that the impact of the salt is reduced.

Sand dune vegetation

Most **sand dunes** have vegetation growing on them. This helps hold the dunes together. Dunes that build high enough can provide shelter for vegetation behind them. A very common sand dune plant is marram grass. Marram grass can deal very well with strong coastal winds. It grows very low to the surface, and its leaves can fold to reduce their surface area. It also has very long roots to reach supplies of water deep under the sand dunes.

Coastal Animals

Many different kinds of animals make their homes along coastlines. Although the animals have to cope with salty water, crashing waves, and high winds, the coast provides rich food and a variety of different **habitats**.

In the **intertidal zone**, animals have **adapted** in many ways. They have adapted to:

- Moisture levels — Sometimes the sea covers the land, at other times it is exposed to the air. Animals must cope with both wet and dry conditions. Animals such as crabs can breathe under the water using **gills**. As long as these gills are kept moist when the crab is out of the water, they can take oxygen from the air and keep the crab alive.
- Moving water — When the tide comes in, powerful waves can crash onto the shore and back again. Animals must be able to withstand this moving water. They do this by burrowing into the sand, like clams, or attaching themselves to rocks, like barnacles.
- Salt water — Some animals have special, thin layers of skin called membranes that can control the amount of salt that passes into the animals' bodies.

▶ Once the tide has gone out, you can see a huge variety of animals that make their homes along the coastline.

Seabirds

Some seabirds, such as the oystercatcher and the egret, are known as wading birds. They are called this because they wade out into the **intertidal zone** and search for worms and molluscs buried in the sand and mud. Other birds live perched on rocky cliffs high above the sea. Here they build nests and raise their young on fish caught in the sea. Gannets have developed an amazing diving technique. They rise into the air and then plunge into the water, catching fish near the surface.

Mammals at the coast

Many different **mammals** live at the coast. Most of them—such as otters, seals, and walruses—spend large parts of their lives in the sea. They come ashore to rest, sleep, give birth, and nurse their pups. Other mammals, such as rabbits and mice, live among the thick coastal vegetation. Rabbits prefer light, sandy coastlines where they can easily dig out burrows.

▲ These kittiwakes and guillemots bring up their young on tiny narrow ledges on the cliff face. They must nest close to the sea so that they can find enough fish to feed their chicks.

Living at the Coast

Humans have settled in coastal areas for thousands of years. There have been huge benefits to living at the coast. The earliest settlements grew up because of the plentiful supply of fish and other seafood found at the coast and in the sea. Also, in some countries, such as Japan, the inland areas are mostly mountainous, so good flat land was found only around the coast.

Later, when sea travel and trade became widespread, it made sense to settle by the coast because goods could be bought and sold there. To help this trade, shipbuilding industries and ports began to grow in coastal areas. This also increased the amount of coastal settlement. A large proportion of today's important cities are on the coast. They have grown from settlements that grew up hundreds of years ago.

Leisure time

Today, the coast is a major attraction for tourists and for local people who like to spend their leisure time there. Industries and companies have taken advantage of this. They have built hotels, apartments, shops, restaurants, and amusements. Many activity companies have set up at the coast, such as diving schools, surfing rental shops, marinas, and boat trip organizations.

▼ Shipping and fishing are still important industries for towns and cities across the world, such as in Hong Kong in China.

Case study — Mombasa

Mombasa is Kenya's largest coastal settlement and second largest city, after Nairobi. It sits in southeastern Kenya on the Indian Ocean coast and has a population of around 500,000 people.

The city grew as an important trade center in the 1500s. At this time the Portuguese had a lot of control over the area, and they built some of Mombasa's famous sites such as Fort Jesus. This fort was used as a trading site, as a prison, and as a way to protect the Portuguese when conflicts with local people arose. After about 200 years, Arab communities in the area took control. Slavery was the main trade out of Mombasa until the 1900s. Spices, cotton, and coffee were also traded.

Today Mombasa is a major tourist destination. The beaches to the north and south of the city are beautiful, and development has been limited to protect some of the natural coastal **habitats**.

▸ Mombasa city center is located on an island on the Kenyan coast.

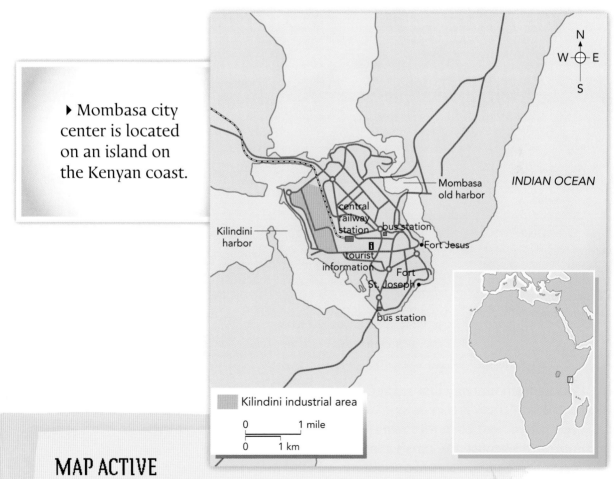

MAP ACTIVE

Why do you think the city grew on an island? What problems might this cause in modern times?

A Way of Life—Iceland

The country of Iceland lies in the northern part of the Atlantic Ocean, between Norway and Greenland. Because the island is very volcanic and mountainous, with large areas covered in glaciers, most of the population of around 300,000 people live around the coast. Iceland's capital city, Reykjavik, is on the southwest coast.

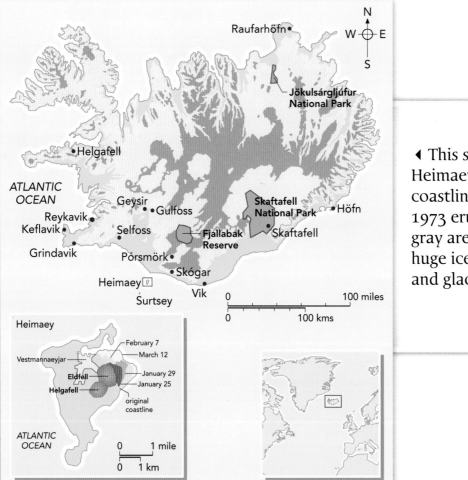

◀ This shows Heimaey's expanding coastline after the 1973 eruption. The gray areas are huge ice sheets and glaciers.

People from Norway first settled in Iceland about 870. In 930 they set up the world's first parliament, called the Althing. Fishing and farming were the main industries in the country's history, although at times food had to be imported because the harsh **climate** made it very difficult to produce food. Today fishing and fish processing are still the main industries. Much of Iceland's international trade is based on its fish and fish products. Around 20 percent of the population work in the fishing industry in some way.

The coastline of Iceland is **evolving**. Iceland sits on top of the Mid-Atlantic Ridge, a huge **faultline** on Earth's surface. This means that volcanic eruptions are frequent. On Heimaey, a small island to the south of the main island, a volcanic eruption in 1973 poured ash and lava over the surface of the island. It eventually ran out to the coast and built a new coastline when the lava cooled. Just a few years earlier, in 1963, an underwater volcano erupted and the lava built up to create a whole new island, called Surtsey.

Today tourism is very important to Iceland. People come to visit the glaciers, the volcanoes, the hot springs, and the beautiful coasts. There are stunning **bays** and **fjords** along the coast, and in the south there are also sandy beaches. The total length of the coastline is almost 3,000 miles (5,000 kilometers).

▲ The inland area of Iceland is mountainous and very cold. Most human settlement and activity in Iceland takes place along the narrow, flat coast of the island.

Our Changing Coasts

Most of our coasts are changing all the time. The sea is an enormously powerful factor in shaping Earth, and coasts are continually being affected. Some dramatic changes are taking place where the sea is **eroding** the coast. These changes can be disastrous, such as when a huge section of sea cliff suddenly collapses after being weakened by **erosion**. This can have devastating results for people who have homes on cliff tops. For example, the Holderness coast on the eastern side of the United Kingdom is badly affected by erosion. The coast is estimated to be retreating by an average of about six feet (two meters) per year. Many cliff-top buildings have fallen into the sea.

▶ Coastal erosion in Bonifacio, Corsica, has left these houses sitting precariously on top of a cliff. One day the cliff may collapse, taking the houses with it.

Rising seas

Rising sea levels is also causing concern for our coasts. A study has shown that sea levels have risen by almost eight inches (20 centimeters) between 1870 and 2004, and that levels will continue to rise in the future. Scientists believe this is because of **global warming**. More heat is being trapped in Earth's atmosphere, which means icebergs, glaciers, and ice caps are melting and running into the sea. Thermal expansion is also taking place, which means that the water increases in volume as it warms. Rising sea levels mean more coastal erosion will take place, and more low-lying coastal areas may soon be flooded.

▼ This map shows the areas of the world that would be flooded if the sea level rose by 330 feet (100 meters).

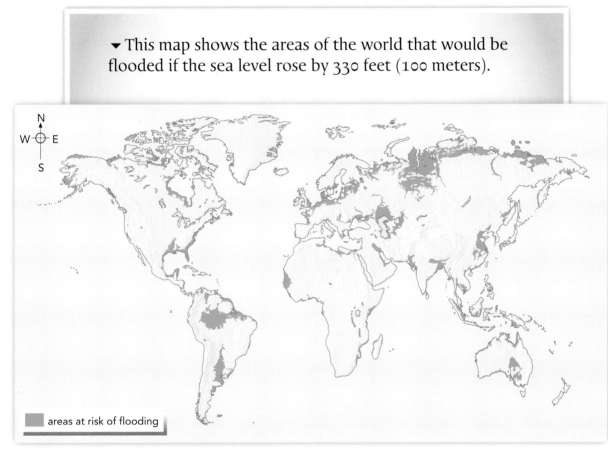

areas at risk of flooding

Is development the answer?

As more and more people want to spend leisure time at the coast, human development is also having an impact. As more roads and buildings are built, more pollution is brought to the coast. Natural coastal **habitats** are cleared to make way for these developments, and the plants and animals that live in them are also lost. Some areas have seen a lot of development. When this happens, the coast often loses the natural beauty that first attracted people to it.

Looking to the Future

Building strong **coastal reinforcements** can reduce coastal **erosion**. There are many different kinds, and they all slow down or stop the erosion of the coast. However, they are expensive and often damage the natural environment. Many scientists now propose a system of **managed retreat** instead. This is where some sections of the coast are allowed to be **eroded** and flooded naturally, while areas where people live and work are protected.

Many coastlines around the world are now protected from too much development. This will help control the pollution and loss of **habitat** at the coast. In addition, looking after the natural coastal habitats is becoming a higher priority for many countries. There have been some terrible shipping disasters in the last 50 years. Oil tankers have spilled their oil into the sea and all over the coast. For example, in March 1989 the *Exxon Valdez* broke up in Prince William Sound, Alaska. Around 10.9 million gallons (41 million liters) of oil spilled into the water. Accidents such as this have made many people very aware of how delicate coastal **ecosystems** can be, and how they need to be protected.

▼ Scandola Nature Reserve is in Cape Porto, Corsica.

▲ Ports continue to play an important role in the world's trade in goods. Victoria Harbor in Hong Kong, China, is one of the world's busiest ports.

Sea change?

Reducing the amount of **carbon dioxide** humans release into the atmosphere will help control **global warming** and the rise in sea levels. In turn, this will help control coastal erosion and prevent some areas from flooding.

Improving the pollution levels of coastal waters would greatly help coastal habitats. Some countries pump untreated sewage directly out into the sea. Stopping this would clean up these areas. Building stronger oil tankers may help reduce the amount of oil spilled in accidents. Dumping some types of waste at sea is illegal, but still some waste is dumped. Reducing this would also help reduce the amount of waste that ends up washing onto coasts.

The coasts are precious resources that provide us with many different opportunities. The coasts are home to a unique range of plants and animals. It is important to take care of our coasts now and in the future.

Coast Facts

Continents and coasts

This table lists the length of coastline for **continents**. Can you think why it might be difficult to measure exactly a continent's coastline length?

Continent	Length of coast in miles (kilometers)
North America	293,635 (472,538)
Europe	202,509 (325,892)
Asia	179,248 (288,459)
Antarctica	96,361 (155,067)
South America	89,833 (144,567)
Australia	85,611 (137,772)
Africa	68,606 (110,406)
World	1,015,803 (1,634,701)

- Seventeen percent of the United Kingdom's coastline is said to be eroding.

- Half of the world's total population lives within 37 miles (60 kilometers) of the coast.

- More than 90 percent of the world's living **biomass** can be found in the oceans and seas.

- More than 3.5 billion people depend on the ocean for their main source of food. In 20 years this number may double to 7 billion.

- An estimated 21 million barrels of oil end up in the oceans every year from street runoff, ships flushing their tanks, and waste from industrial facilities.

- An average of 600,000 barrels of oil have accidentally spilled from ships into the ocean each year over the last decade.

Find Out More

Further reading

Morris, Neil. *Landscapes and People: Earth's Changing Coasts*. Chicago: Raintree, 2003.

Woodward, John. *Exploring the Oceans: Tidal Zone*. Chicago: Heinemann Library, 2004.

Steele, Phillip. *Earth's Changing Landscape: Changing Coastlines*. New York, NY: Franklin Watts, 2003.

Web sites

www.epa.gov/owow/oceans/kids.html
This Environmental Protection Agency site looks at oceans, coasts, and estuaries.

www.nationalgeographic.com/geographyaction/habitats/oceans_coasts.html
This site looks at ocean and coastal habitats, with photo galleries and online adventures.

Map Active answers

Page 6: There are no large cities near the coast in the northern parts of the world. This is because most of these places have very harsh winters, and the sea can freeze, making it difficult for trade to come in and out on ships. Also, fewer people live in these cold areas, so there are hardly any large cities.

Page 21: Mombasa probably grew on an island because it was easier for the Portuguese to defend themselves against local people on an island, where any attacks would have to be made by boat. However, for modern life, there may be a problem with road traffic. There is only one bridge linking the south of the island to the mainland, so all road traffic must come through this area. This may cause huge congestion in the area.

Glossary

abrasion erosion caused by moving stones carried by wind or water

adapted changed to suit certain conditions

arch coastal feature formed when a cave is eroded right through to the other side, creating a large hole through the rock (an archway)

bar area of sand and shingle deposited along the coast, forming a long section of land that joins the coast

barrier island long, thin island made of deposited sand and shingle, running parallel to the coastline

bay sheltered section of coast, often almost enclosed by areas of harder rock, where soft rock has been eroded

beach replenishment moving large amounts of beach material (sand, shingle, and stones) to areas of the coast where material is being eroded away

biomass combined weight of living plants and animals

carbon dioxide gas that is released by burning fossil fuels (coal, oil, and gas) and that traps heat in Earth's atmosphere

cell tiny building block that makes up the bodies of plants and animals

climate rainfall, temperature, and wind that normally affect a large area over a long period of time

coastal reinforcement protecting the coast against erosion using man-made barriers that absorb the eroding energy of the sea

compressed squashed to a high pressure

continent any one of the world's largest continuous land masses

corrosion when something is gradually eaten away, for example through being dissolved by chemicals

deposition where water drops its load of rock and silt

ecosystem set of relationships between different plants and animals living together in a habitat

erode wear away by wind, water, ice, or acid

erosion wearing away of rocks and soil by wind, water, ice, or chemicals

evolve when, over a long period of time, animals and plants develop features and habitats that help them survive in their environment

faultline large crack in Earth's surface, often where two giant plates of Earth's crust meet

fetch maximum distance of open water over which the wind can blow before reaching the coast

fjord long, narrow mountain valley, carved by a glacier, which reaches the coast and has been flooded by the sea

gill organ on animals living in water that takes in oxygen from the water

global warming gradual (slow) increase in temperature that affects the whole Earth

gravity force that pulls all objects toward Earth

habitat place where a plant or animal usually grows or lives

halophyte plant that can cope with salty growing conditions

headland area of hard rock that is more resistant to erosion than the surrounding softer rock, leaving the hard rock sticking out into the sea

high tide highest point every day where the sea reaches up the shore

hydraulic pressure force exerted by a liquid, like sea water, against something

interaction how two things behave toward and affect each other

intertidal zone area of shore between the high tide and low tide marks

landlocked surrounded by land, with no coast

longshore drift movement of beach material (sand, shingle, and stones) along the coast by the action of waves

low tide lowest point every day where the sea moves down the shore

mammal animal that feeds its young with its own milk

managed retreat allowing some sections of coast to erode while protecting other areas

mudflat area of land formed by deposited mud and silt

salt marsh area of low-lying silt and mud around the coast where certain types of salt-tolerant plants can grow

sand dune sandy ridge or hill found at the top of a beach, above the high tide mark, formed from wind-blown sand

shingle small rounded stones found at the coast and formed by waves eroding larger stones

silt fine particles of eroded rock and soil that can settle in along the coast, sometimes blocking the movement of water

species smallest grouping used to classify animals. The members of a species are very similar to one another and can mate to produce young.

spit long, narrow area of land formed by deposited sand and shingle, joined to the coast at one end only

stack tower of rock left sticking up out of the sea, created when the roof of an arch collapses

tide rise and fall in the surface of the sea, caused by the pull of the Moon's gravity

tide pool small body of water left behind in rocks when the tide goes out

tombolo stretch of deposited sand or shingle that joins an island to the mainland

wave pounding force of water hitting a rock and sending shock waves through the rock

wave-cut platform section of rock created when cliffs above sea level collapse due to erosion by waves

Index